Fun With Fabric F

The projects in this book take their inspiration from the German art form "scherenschnitte" (shair-en-shnit-teh) or scissor cutting. If you ever made lacy Valentines from paper folded in half, snowflakes from paper folded multiple times, or rows of doll figures holding hands, you have practiced "scherenschnitte."

We have taken the idea of folding then cutting paper and adapted it to fabric. We scissor-cut the fabric to create frames for wall quilts and individual quilt blocks that feature patchwork, embroidery, appliqué or novelty fabric motifs. Our frames also appear on Christmas stockings and home-decor items.

The frames are small-to-large in size and include a multitude of design styles. In many cases the center fabric pieces left over from cutting out the fabric frames are utilized to make secondary frames.

Our fabric frames make a unique and attractive way to highlight designs and create attractive borders. Just about any fabric can be used for frames, which can be sewn to the background by hand or machine. We have utilized a variety of frame fabrics—directional prints, florals, novelty prints, tone on tones, etc.—so you can see the effects each provides. The frame fabric can highlight a design or reinforce the theme of the design.

We hope you enjoy our idea of fabric frames. We have had fun creating the wide range of projects in this book to provide something for everyone.

Meet the Designers

Joyce Mori

Joyce has authored 15 books and written over 75 articles on various quilting subjects. She has a line of stencils with Quilting Stencils International, and her line of Native American inspired patterns are found at Southwest Decoratives.

The National Quilting Association awarded Joyce a grant to study the use of Native American designs on quilts. Her quilts have appeared in many galleries, exhibits and shows, and she teaches at guilds and conferences throughout the United States.

Joyce has a Ph.D. from the University of Missouri. Her husband is recently retired, and they live in central Illinois. She has one married daughter.

Pat Hill

Pat has been quilting for 30 years and teaching quilting for 20 years. She enjoys giving trunk shows and lectures at quilt guilds. Her quilts have been published in *Quilter's Newsletter Magazine, NQA Patchwork Patter, British Patchwork & Quilting* and other publications.

Besides quilting, Pat's hobbies include gardening and training dogs. Now that she is a grandmother, she has slowed down a bit and only completes about two quilts per month. Her background experience includes 10 years of teaching high school and five years of teaching grammar school.

General Instructions

Most of the projects in this book share the same basic techniques. Refer to these General Instructions as needed to complete the various projects.

Our projects provide specific sizes for the frame and its background. However, you can take our frame designs and reduce or enlarge them, perhaps with modifications, to fit any background you might want to use.

These basic instructions take you through the steps used to create a frame for a 12½"-square block (finished size 12"). We have used a three-fold design. Some patterns in the book feature single- or double-fold designs.

Note: *Please read all instructions before starting a project.*

You will need the following:
- Background fabric (A)
  This could be a patchwork-pieced block or a block with an appliqué design, a novelty print, a block with an embroidery motif, etc.
- 14" square of the frame fabric (B)
- 12" square of fusible web
- 12½" square tear-away fabric stabilizer
- 12" square paper for the pattern

Additional supplies needed:
- Appliqué pressing cloth
- Machine-appliqué thread to match or contrast with your frame fabric
  A contrasting color emphasizes the design of the frame against the background. The choice is personal preference based on the final effect you wish to achieve.
- Flat-head straight pins
- Basic sewing supplies and tools

INSTRUCTIONS
Making the Pattern
1. Select and trace a pattern from this book onto a piece of paper and cut it out. Transfer marks or notes to the templates. **Note:** *The samples and instructions given here use a 12" finished frame. Refer to the project instructions for sizes for background and pattern pieces.*

2. Fold the 12" square of paper in half and in half again. Then fold in half again on the diagonal as shown in Figure 1. **Note:** *Keep the outside edges of the folded paper together and the folded edges together.*

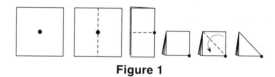

Figure 1

3. Hold the folded paper in place with a few straight pins as shown below. **Note:** *For some projects the pattern is presented as half of the square, so you fold only once; or as one quarter of the square, so you fold twice. In some cases the entire pattern is provided so there is no folding. The example shown has a diagonal fold, which is a pattern with the most folds.*

4. Draw the pattern on the 12" square of folded paper as shown.

HOUSE OF WHITE BIRCHES, BERNE, INDIANA 46711 • DRGNETWORK.COM

5. Cut out the frame pattern. Open out the folds and see how the paper frame fits your selected background fabric. **_Note:_** _This step helps you determine where to cut your background piece. You do not want important parts of the background motif to be covered, so keep moving the frame template as needed._ Cut out a 12" x 12" A background square.

6. If the frame is suitable for your background, trace around the paper pattern on the paper side of the fusible web. Use straight pins if needed to hold the template in place.

7. Center the square of fusible web on the wrong side of the frame fabric B square. **_Note:_** _The B square will be larger than the fusible web._ Fuse it in place with an iron referring to the manufacturer's instructions.

8. Use a rotary cutter to make a small slit somewhere along the inside design line. Insert scissors into the slit and cut the frame in one piece, leaving the center in one piece also as shown.

9. Remove the paper backing from the frame section.

10. Lay the frame fusible side up on your ironing board. Center the A background square right side down on the frame.

11. Fuse the frame to the background, using an appliqué pressing cloth, if necessary, to keep from getting any portion of the fusible web on your iron.

12. Pin the square of tear-away stabilizer to the wrong side of the fused frame.

13. Machine-appliqué the inside of the frame to the background. **_Note:_** _If you use a buttonhole stitch, it takes less time and uses less thread. A satin stitch defines the frame more but takes more time and thread. The choice is a personal preference. You may use thread to match the frame or a contrasting thread to emphasize the frame._

14. Trim block to size specified in the project instructions, leaving approximately ¼" beyond the edges of the background square all around.

THE CUTOUT CENTER OF THE FRAME FABRIC

When each frame is cut out, there is a center portion that is not used for the main project. This piece has the fusible web in place if it was leftover from a project made using the machine-appliqué technique.

These fused fabric centers can usually be used to make additional frames for smaller projects.

USING LEFTOVER CENTERS

The basic concept for using the leftover centers of frames is to keep cutting designs from the center. The first cut, and sometimes the only cut one can make if the center is really small, is one that will produce a frame with decorated outside edges and straight edges on the interior of the frame. This is exactly opposite of the first frame which has a decorated inside and straight edges on the outside.

Using the Leftover Center Piece

1. Fold the cutout fabric in half on the diagonal with paper side out; pin with straight pins to secure.

2. Fold in half again and crease to mark the center. Measure up 4½" from the center toward the point and mark. Measure 4½" on each side of the drawn line along the folded edge and mark; draw a diagonal line from these marks to the center point as shown. ***Note:*** *You may select any*

size you wish for this open area in the center to showcase your fabric's design.

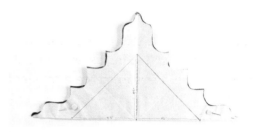

3. Cut on the drawn solid lines.

4. Remove pins and open to reveal another frame with a smaller center opening.

5. Select a background and fuse the frame in place. ***Note:*** *All outside and inside edges of the frame must be appliquéd in place. Part of the background must extend beyond the frame to allow for seam allowance. You can allow any size border around the frame that you wish, just remember to allow for seam allowances.*

6. The cutout square leftover in step 4 may be used to create even smaller frames. Begin by folding the square in half and in half again.

7. Using the C pattern provided on page 7, draw a new design on the inside and cut out the frame as in previous steps to create a smaller frame. Then using the cutout center again and following steps 1–4, make another even smaller frame as shown below. Fuse these to backgrounds.

USES FOR THE FRAMES

The frames are perfect for making mini quilts to hang as little decorations in an office cubicle, on the fridge, on a bulletin board or on a Christmas tree or given as gifts.

The frames may be converted into recipe-card frames or used as mug mats or coasters. Some of the projects shown here feature a picture of the leftover center area used in another item.

GENERAL INSTRUCTIONS FOR A MINI QUILT

You will not need fusible web because it is already in place since the frame is being cut from a leftover center section.

If you are making a frame that has a straight outside edge, cut the background fabric ¼" smaller on all sides than the frame.

If you are using a frame that has curved edges on the outside, cut the background ⅜"–¾" larger on all sides than the frame. This allows ¼" for seam allowances and the remainder for a narrow border.

1. Fuse the frame to the background.

2. Cut backing and a piece of batting the same size as the background fabric with frame.

3. Lay the frame/background right side up. Layer the backing on top of this, wrong side up. Place the batting on top; pin the layers together.

4. Sew around all outside edges using a ¼" seam allowance, leaving an opening for turning; trim the corners.

5. Turn right side out; fold opening edges to the inside and hand-stitch the opening closed. Press flat; machine-quilt as desired.

6. Add a hanger if needed.

MORE USES FOR LEFTOVER CENTERS

A second method for using the leftover centers is very easy and allows you to make larger quilts.

The whole center is appliquéd onto a background block. In the examples shown, an additional motif is appliquéd on the top of the leftover center. Such a motif serves to reinforce the theme of the quilt.

TWO FRAMES ARE MORE FUN THAN ONE

If one frame is good, two frames are even better. The quilt below uses all the leftover frames from the original quilt on a whole-cloth background.

More Fun with Frames by Pat Hill

You may add a frame to the outside of a frame to set it off from a background as shown in Buffalo Crossing. Additional buffalo motifs were cut

from the fabric and appliquéd to a couple of the leftover centers to add interest to the design.

Buffalo Crossing by Pat Hill

Another way to make a larger quilt is to combine framed units with pieced or appliquéd blocks. In How Does Your Garden Grow, Pat Hill combines circular frames with Nine-Patch blocks to create a fabric garden.

How Does Your Garden Grow by Pat Hill.

Many ways to use this framing method are included with the instructions for specific projects given in this book. Once you have made a few projects using this framing method, you will find yourself thinking of other ways to incorporate frames in your future quilts. As you try this technique and create your own frame projects, please note that you can begin with a frame and select a motif to fit into the frame area, or you can create your center motif and then make a frame to surround it.

Have fun expanding your quilting horizons as you create your own fabric frames.

FINISHING THE QUILTED PROJECT

1. Sandwich the batting between the completed top and prepared backing; pin, baste or spray-baste to hold.

2. Quilt as desired; remove pins or basting, if used. Trim batting and backing even with the top.

3. Join the binding strips on short ends with diagonal seams to make a long strip; press seams to one side.

4. Press under ¼" on one long edge of the binding strip.

5. Pin and stitch raw edge of binding to the raw edge of the quilted top, mitering corners and overlapping ends. Fold binding to the back side and stitch in place to finish.

GENERAL APPLIQUÉ INSTRUCTIONS

You may choose to hand- or machine-appliqué the frames to the backgrounds.

Machine Appliqué

1. Trace pattern on paper; cut out.

2. Fold the fusible-web square to fit the cutout pattern. Trace the pattern onto the paper side of the fusible web.

3. Center and fuse the frame to the wrong side of the framing fabric; cut out on traced lines. Remove paper backing.

4. Fuse the cutout fabric frame onto the right side of the background fabric.

5. Place tear-away fabric stabilizer on the wrong side of the fused background fabric.

6. Satin-stitch or buttonhole/blanket-stitch around the frame edges by machine using matching or contrasting thread.

7. Remove fabric stabilizer.

Hand Appliqué

1. Trace design on the matte side of a freezer-paper square folded to fit pattern.

2. Center and iron the shiny side of the freezer paper on the right side of the frame fabric.

3. Cut out the frame ³⁄₁₆" away from paper edge of frame.

4. Pin, baste or spray-baste the cutout frame onto the background.

5. Turn under the inside edge of the frame even with the freezer-paper pattern edge; remove freezer paper.

6. Hand-stitch frame in place on background. ■

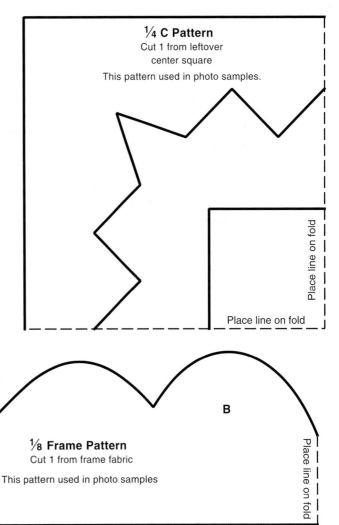

¼ **C Pattern**
Cut 1 from leftover
center square
This pattern used in photo samples.

Place line on fold

Place line on fold

⅛ **Frame Pattern**
Cut 1 from frame fabric
This pattern used in photo samples

B

Place line on fold

Place line on fold

Outside edge

Whimsical Flowers

BY JOYCE MORI

A folk-art design with a modern twist is featured on this whimsical wall quilt.

PROJECT NOTES

This wall quilt is framed at the corners to imitate the old photo corners found in antique photo albums or scrapbooks. The corner motifs are similar in value and color to the outer border so they visually blend to create a larger frame. The appliquéd flowers are framed with hand embroidery to provide embellishment on the center panel.

PROJECT SPECIFICATIONS

Quilt Size: 22" x 22"

MATERIALS

- 1 (18" x 18") A square gold tonal
- Fat quarter black print for flowers
- 8" square green print for leaves
- 1 fat quarter gray/green print
- 2 strips each 2½" x 15½" B and 2½" x 19½" C pale yellow print
- 2 strips each 2" x 19½" D and 2" x 22½" E gray tonal
- 100" (1⅛"-wide) black/gray stripe binding strip
- Batting 25" x 25"
- Backing 25" x 25"
- All-purpose thread to match fabrics
- Clear nylon monofilament thread for quilting
- Rust embroidery floss
- 1 yard fusible web
- 1 yard fabric stabilizer
- Pattern paper
- Basic sewing tools and supplies

INSTRUCTIONS

1. Refer to the General Instructions to prepare, fuse and appliqué the four flower/leaf motifs to A. **Note:** *This pattern is not a complete frame; it frames each corner. The pattern paper should be folded only once diagonally.*

2. Transfer the embroidery design to A and hand-embroider a running stitch along the lines using 3 strands of rust floss.

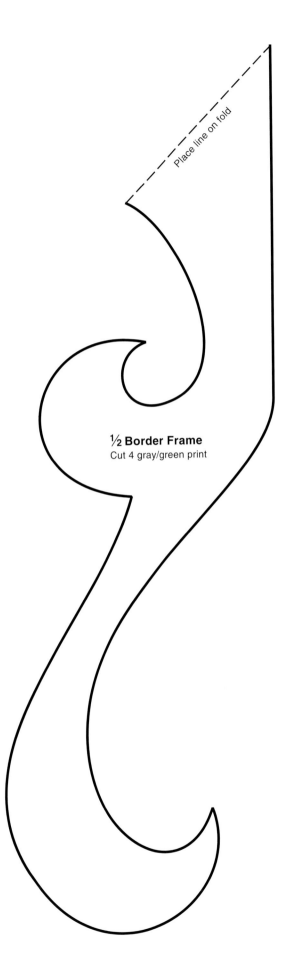

Place line on fold

½ **Border Frame**
Cut 4 gray/green print

3. Trim the stitched block to 15½" x 15½".

4. Sew B strips to opposite sides and C strips to the remaining sides of A; press seams toward B and C.

5. Prepare and apply frame motifs to the B and C strips using pattern given and referring to the General Instructions and Figure 1.

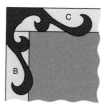

Figure 1

6. Sew the D strips to the B sides and E strips to the C sides of A to complete the top; press seams toward D and E strips.

7. Complete the quilt referring to page 6. ■

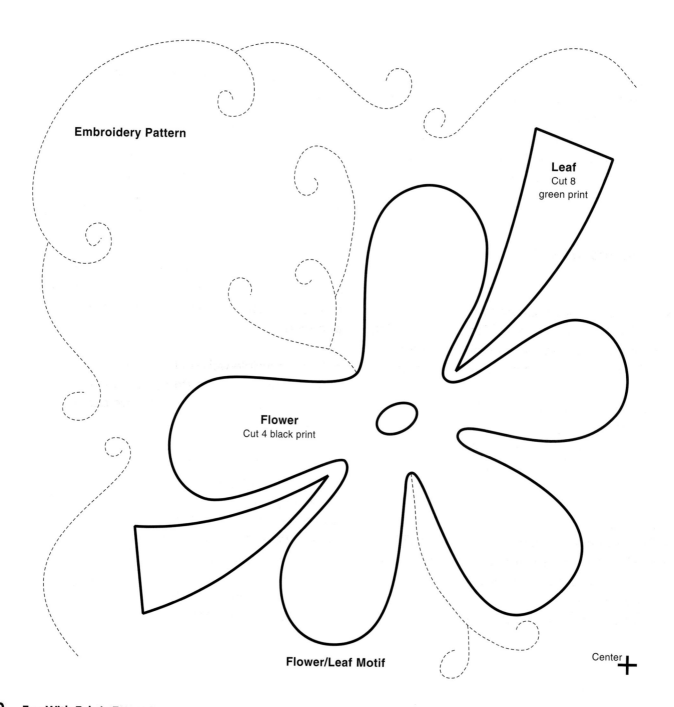

Embroidery Pattern

Leaf
Cut 8
green print

Flower
Cut 4 black print

Flower/Leaf Motif

Center

Native American Pottery Quilt

BY JOYCE MORI

This design from a Southwestern pottery piece makes a striking center for a wall quilt.

PROJECT NOTES

The frame used to border the embroidery pot is cut in four separate pieces. This type of frame works well when you may not have enough of a fabric to cut the frame as a whole unit. Another instance where this works best is if you want to use a stripe fabric as a frame and you want the stripe to run parallel to the project edges.

PROJECT SPECIFICATIONS

Finished Size: 18" x 18"

MATERIALS

- 15" x 15" A square cream tonal
- 4 (3" x 14") strips each multicolor ombré print, fusible web and tear-away fabric stabilizer
- 2 (2" x 12") B strips and 2 (2" x 15") C strips cream solid
- 2 (2½" x 15") D strips and 2 (2½" x 20") E strips tan solid
- 82" (1⅛"-wide) rust mottled binding strip
- Backing 24" x 24"
- Batting 24" x 24"
- All-purpose thread to match or contrast with fabrics
- Clear nylon monofilament thread for quilting
- Black, medium gray, rust, medium brown and medium tan embroidery floss
- Pattern paper
- Basic sewing tools and supplies

INSTRUCTIONS

1. Center and trace the pottery motif onto the A square.

2. Using 3 strands of embroidery floss, outline-stitch all marked lines except for the two side motifs, which feature a running stitch.

3. Trim the embroidered A square to 11½" x 11½" after stitching.

4. Sew B–E border strips to the top and bottom and then the sides of the embroidered center in alphabetical order; press seams toward strips as added.

5. Iron the fusible-web strips to the wrong side of the multicolor ombré strips; trace the frame design on the strips. Cut out; remove paper backing.

6. Referring to Figure 1, place a strip with the top edge of the longer frame section aligned with seam between the A square and the bottom B border strips; trim the ends of the strip at the seam between the B and C border strips. Fuse strip in place.

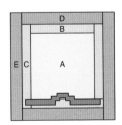

Figure 1

Repeat on top of the A square.

7. Align the remaining strips with the seams between the A square and the side C border strips; trim ends even with the outer edge of the fused frame strips, if necessary. Fuse in place.

8. Machine-appliqué frame pieces in place referring to the General Instructions.

9. Complete the quilt referring to page 6. ◾

Place line on fold

Pottery Pattern

Native American Frame
Cut 4 multicolor ombré print

Afternoon Delight

BY PAT HILL

Select design motifs from pretty prints to cut and appliqué to a background and frame to make a personalized wall quilt.

PROJECT SPECIFICATIONS
Finished Size: 18¼" x 18¼"

MATERIALS
- 4 (6¼" x 6¼") A squares light blue mottled
- 4 (8" x 8") B squares and 2 (10" x 10") D squares blue multicolor print
- 2 (10" x 10") squares gold tonal; cut each square in half on one diagonal to make 4 C triangles
- 4 (6¼" x 6¼") squares and 2 (11" x 11") squares each fusible web and tear-away fabric stabilizer
- 4 each fussy-cut teapot and rose motifs to fit on A and C (add seam allowance all around when cutting for hand-appliqué, if desired)
- 85" (1⅛"-wide) gold tonal binding strip
- Backing 22" x 22"
- Batting 22" x 22"
- All-purpose thread to match or contrast with fabrics
- Clear nylon monofilament thread for quilting
- Pattern paper
- Basic sewing tools and supplies

INSTRUCTIONS
1. Hand- or machine-appliqué teapot motifs to A and rose motifs to C referring to the General Appliqué Instructions on page 7.

2. Prepare B frame pieces and apply to A squares referring to the General Instructions; trim blocks to 6¾" x 6¾".

3. Join two blocks to make a row; repeat. Press seams in opposite directions; join rows and press.

4. Sew a C triangle to each side of the pieced center; press seams toward C.

5. Cut the D squares and large fusible-web squares in half on one diagonal. Fold the fusible-web triangles in half with paper side out as shown in Figure 1; draw the D frame design (on page 40) onto the paper side and cut out.

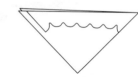

Figure 1

6. Remove paper backing; fuse to the wrong side of the D triangles. Cut out corner frames.

7. Fuse a frame piece to each C corner triangle; trim ends to butt against adjacent frames, if necessary.

8. Quilt and bind referring to page 6. ∎

Templates continued on page 40.

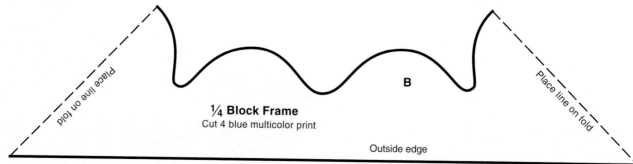

Place line on fold

¼ **Block Frame**
Cut 4 blue multicolor print

B

Place line on fold

Outside edge

Frame It!

BY JOYCE MORI

Frame your favorite photos with fabrics to enhance the theme of the photo.

PROJECT NOTES

You can make frames to reflect holidays or themes such as hobbies, weddings, baby pictures, etc. So make some up as gifts for your friends and relatives. The size is adjustable; you only have to remember that the center cutout part of the frame must be smaller than the photograph by ¼" on all sides. This overlap of the fabric frame on the photo keeps it from falling out of the frame.

PROJECT SPECIFICATIONS

Finished Size: 7½" x 9½"

MATERIALS

- 1 (10½" x 8½") A background piece
- 2 (10" x 8") rectangles B frame fabric
- 1 (9½" x 7½") rectangle each fusible web, very stiff interfacing and backing fabric
- 1 (6½" x 4½") rectangle each fusible web and card stock
- All-purpose thread to match or contrast with fabrics
- Water-soluble stabilizer
- Pattern paper
- Basic sewing tools and supplies

INSTRUCTIONS

1. Iron the fusible web to the wrong side of one of the frame fabric rectangles; remove paper backing. Fuse the wrong side of second frame piece to it to make doubled-layer frame fabric with a right side on both front and back.

2. Trace the frame pattern onto paper; cut out the pattern except for the center. Trace the pattern onto the frame fabric; cut out the frame.

3. Cut the center from the paper pattern. Test that the center cut out from the paper pattern is ¼" smaller on all sides than the photograph. **Note:** If your print is 4" x 6", you need an opening 3½" x 5½".

4. Satin-stitch around the center opening of the frame. **Note**: Use water-soluble stabilizer for this since normal stabilizer leaves little fuzzies on the edge when it is torn away. Follow the directions on the package.

5. Iron fusible web to one side of the card-stock rectangle; cut out the center. The center is formed by drawing a line ¼" in from the outside edges. Remove the paper from the card frame; fuse to the underside of the frame to provide additional stability to the opening edges of the frame.

6. Center the frame on the background fabric; machine-appliqué the frame to the background around only the outer edges. Do not appliqué the center cut-out area.

7. Place the frame wrong side up on a flat surface; center the piece of stiff interfacing on top. Finally, add the backing right side up. Pin all layers together. Bring the outside edge of the background fabric to the back. Fold under ¼" and pin this down; hand-stitch in place on the back to finish edge.

8. Machine-quilt around the outside edge of the frame with monofilament thread.

9. Place your photo in the center of the frame. **Note:** If the photo slides down, add a piece of

HOUSE OF WHITE BIRCHES, BERNE, INDIANA 46711   DRGNETWORK.COM

double-sided tape to the back side to secure it to the fabric. Add a hanging device such as a magnet, hanging sleeve or ring. ▨

¼ Frame
Cut 1 from double-layer frame fabric

Place line on fold

Place line on fold

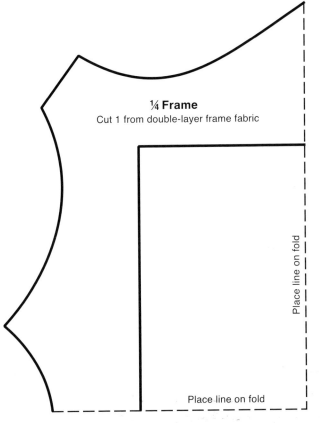

Wild Cats

BY JOYCE MORI

A cat print is featured in the frames of this wall quilt.

PROJECT NOTES

An allover print can be framed to highlight the print motifs. In this project, the cats are the featured design. Any type of theme print would work perfectly in this kind of frame including children's, holiday or seasonal prints.

A second version of this design uses several different Southwestern-theme prints that were fussy-cut to fit the frame openings as shown above. The corner accents on the Wild Cats project (shown on page 19) simulate the corner frames used in old photo albums.

PROJECT SPECIFICATIONS

Finished Size: 19" x 19"

MATERIALS

- 4 (8" x 8") A squares each cat print (A), fusible web and tear-away fabric stabilizer
- 4 (10" x 10") B squares purple tonal
- 4 (5" x 5") squares each turquoise tonal (C), fusible web and tear-away fabric stabilizer
- 2 (2½" x 2½") H squares turquoise tonal
- 2 strips each 1½" x 8½" D and 1½" x 17½" E black-and-white print
- 2 strips each 1½" x 17½" F and 1½" x 19½" G black solid
- 88" (1⅛"-wide) black solid binding strip
- Backing 22" x 22"
- Batting 22" x 22"
- All-purpose thread to match or contrast with fabrics
- Clear nylon monofilament thread for quilting
- Pattern paper
- Basic sewing tools and supplies

INSTRUCTIONS

1. Prepare and cut frame pattern and corner accent pieces as directed on patterns.

2. Refer to the General Instructions to frame each A square with B referring to Figure 1; trim blocks to 8½" x 8½".

3. Join two blocks with D, again referring to Figure 1; press seams toward D. Repeat and join the rows with E; press seams toward E.

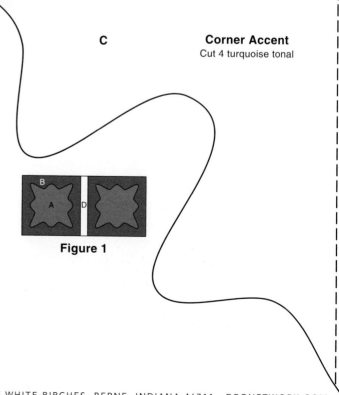

C

Corner Accent
Cut 4 turquoise tonal

Figure 1

HOUSE OF WHITE BIRCHES, BERNE, INDIANA 46711 DRGNETWORK.COM

4. Sew F to opposite sides and G to the top and bottom; press seams toward strips.

5. Layer H squares right sides together; sew all around. Cut a slit in one square and turn right side out through the slit; press.

6. Center the stitched H unit to the center referring to the project photo for positioning.

7. Arrange, fuse and stitch a corner accent piece to each corner referring to the General Instructions to complete the top.

8. Complete the quilt referring to page 6. ■

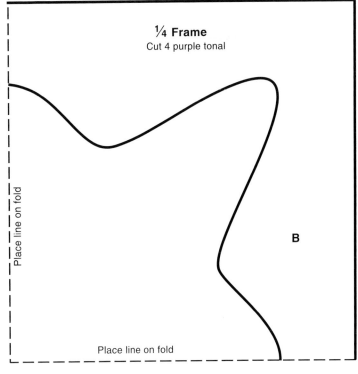

¼ Frame
Cut 4 purple tonal

Place line on fold

B

Place line on fold

Four Flowers Table Mat

BY JOYCE MORI

Beautiful flowers are the main attraction in this pretty mat.

PROJECT SPECIFICATIONS
Finished Size: 15" x 15"

MATERIALS
- 4 (6" x 6") squares each floral print (A), fusible web and tear-away fabric stabilizer
- 4 (8" x 8") B squares each navy/black print, fusible web and tear-away fabric stabilizer
- 2 strips each 1" x 12½" C and 1" x 13½" D bright pink tonal
- 2 strips each 1½" x 13½" E and 1½" x 15½" F navy tonal
- 72" (1⅛"-wide) navy solid binding strip
- Backing 18" x 18"
- Batting 18" x 18"
- All-purpose thread to match or contrast with fabrics
- Clear nylon monofilament thread for quilting
- Pattern paper
- Basic sewing tools and supplies

INSTRUCTIONS
1. Prepare and cut frame pattern as directed on pattern.

2. Refer to the General Instructions to frame each A square with B referring to Figure 1; trim blocks to 6½" x 6½".

Figure 1

3. Join two blocks to make a row; press. Repeat. Join the rows to complete the center.

4. Sew C strips to opposite sides and D strips to the top and bottom; press seams toward D and C strips. Repeat with E and F strips to complete the pieced top referring to Figure 2.

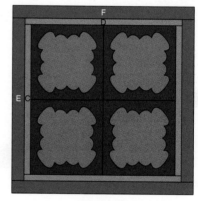

Figure 2

5. Complete the quilt referring to page 6. ■

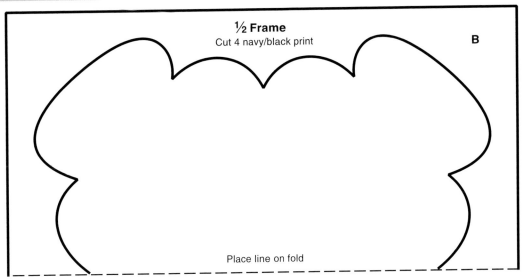

½ Frame
Cut 4 navy/black print

B

Place line on fold

Tulip Intrigue

BY JOYCE MORI

A tulip print is double-framed in this small quilted project.

PROJECT NOTES

The center frame of this small project features a stylized tulip flower showcasing a tulip print. A careful look at the center frame shows satin stitching that serves to separate the flower from its leaves.

The ornate satin-stitched frame serves to create a leaf motif at the base of the flower. It is as if the tulips are partially hidden by overgrown vegetation.

PROJECT SPECIFICATIONS

Finished Size: 10" x 10"

MATERIALS

- 1 (6" x 6") square each tulip print (A), fusible web and tear-away fabric stabilizer
- 1 (7" x 7") square green print B
- 1 (12" x 12") C square floral print
- 1 (10" x 10") square each fusible web and tear-away fabric stabilizer
- 2 strips each 2½" x 6½" D and 2½" x 10½" E lavender scroll print
- 52" (1⅛"-wide) pink/purple print binding strip
- Backing 14" x 14"
- Batting 14" x 14"
- All-purpose thread to match or contrast with fabrics
- Clear nylon monofilament thread for quilting
- Pattern paper
- Basic sewing tools and supplies

INSTRUCTIONS

1. Prepare and cut frame patterns as directed on pattern.

Into the Garden This block centers a garden gate in the center of the flower. The dark blue outer frame adds to the mystery of what is in the garden.

Modern Art The leftover center from Into the Garden is used to create a modern-art design. This would fit perfectly in an office cubicle.

HOUSE OF WHITE BIRCHES, BERNE, INDIANA 46711   DRGNETWORK.COM

2. Refer to the General Instructions to frame the A square with B referring to Figure 1; trim the unit to 6½" x 6½".

Figure 1

3. Sew D strips to opposite sides and E strips to the top and bottom; press seams toward D and E strips.

4. Center the C frame on the framed A-B center as shown in Figure 2; fuse and machine-appliqué in place.

5. Center and trim project to 10½" x 10½".

6. Complete the quilt referring to page 6. ■

Figure 2

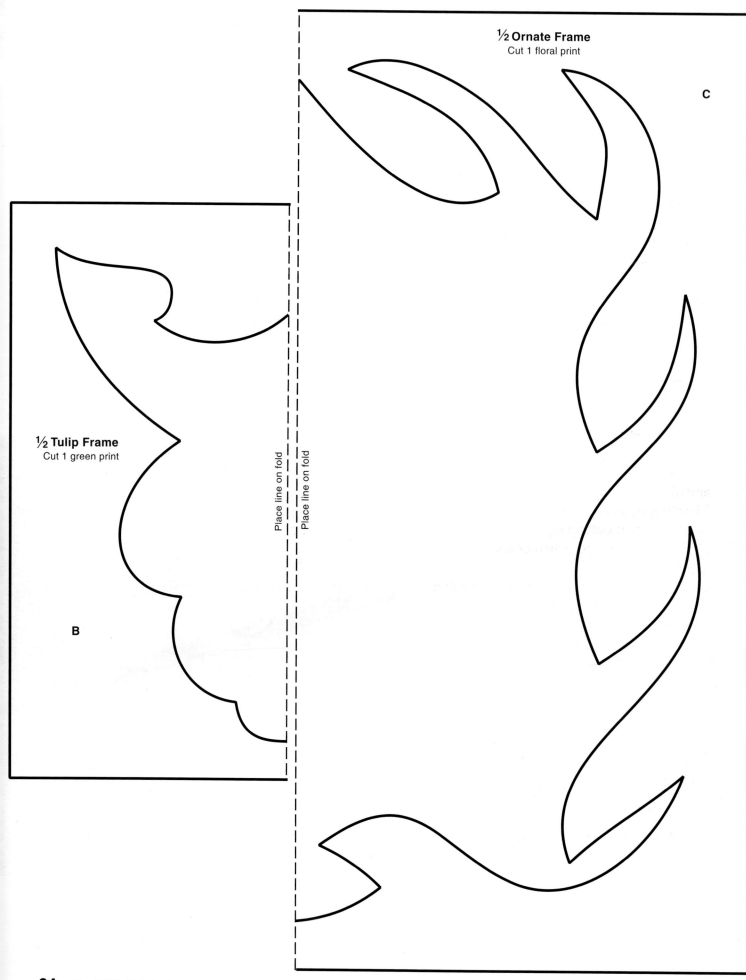

½ **Ornate Frame**
Cut 1 floral print

C

½ **Tulip Frame**
Cut 1 green print

Place line on fold

Place line on fold

B

HOUSE OF WHITE BIRCHES, BERNE, INDIANA 46711   DRGNETWORK.COM

Framed Hot Mats

BY JOYCE MORI

Hand-embroidered centers are framed with free-form designs to make a set of pretty hot mats.

PROJECT SPECIFICATIONS
Finished Size: 9" x 9"

MATERIALS
- 2 (10" x 10") A squares lavender tonal
- 1 (12" x 12") B square each purple stripe and blue batik
- 2 (7½" x 7½") squares each fusible web and tear-away fabric stabilizer
- 2 strips each 1¼" x 8" C and 1¼" x 9½" D navy and dark blue mottleds
- 2 backing squares 9½" x 9½"
- 2 heat-resistant batting squares 9½" x 9½"
- All-purpose thread to match or contrast with fabrics
- Clear nylon monofilament thread for quilting
- Embroidery floss in choice of colors
- Pattern paper
- Basic sewing tools and supplies

INSTRUCTIONS
1. Transfer embroidery designs to A; stitch on the marked lines using 2 strands of embroidery floss in desired colors and an outline or running stitch to complete the embroidery.

2. Center design and trim A squares to 7½" x 7½".

3. Prepare B frame pieces and apply to embroidered A squares referring to the General Instructions on page 2; trim blocks to 8" x 8".

4. Select matching fabric C and D strips; sew C strips to opposite sides and D strips to the top and bottom of each block; press seams toward C and D strips.

5. Finish hot mats referring to making a mini quilt in the General Instructions. ■

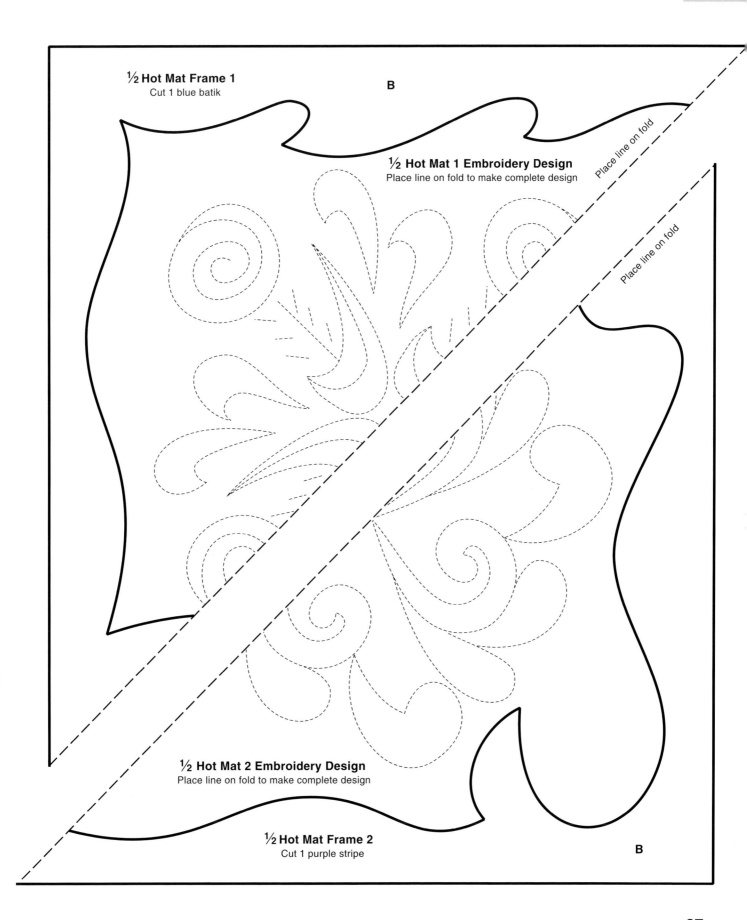

½ **Hot Mat Frame 1**
Cut 1 blue batik

B

½ **Hot Mat 1 Embroidery Design**
Place line on fold to make complete design

Place line on fold

Place line on fold

½ **Hot Mat 2 Embroidery Design**
Place line on fold to make complete design

½ **Hot Mat Frame 2**
Cut 1 purple stripe

B

Quickie Coasters

BY JOYCE MORI

For a quick gift stitch, consider these frame coasters.

PROJECT NOTES

Make two coasters by cutting two frames from the same frame fabric square (see page 4 of the General Instructions).

Select a background that reflects a hobby or interest such as gardening, travel, antiques, seasonal or pets. A set of coasters can reflect any subject. These make perfect hostess gifts—everyone needs coasters.

There are two small drawings inside each frame pattern. Style A shows the first frame piece on a background square; style B uses the cut-out center from style A to make a second frame piece on a square of the same background fabric.

PROJECT SPECIFICATIONS

Finished Size: 4½" x 4½" or 6" x 6"

MATERIALS

- 2 (4½" x 4½" or 6" x 6") A squares background fabric
- 2 (5" x 5" or 6½" x 6½") B squares frame fabric
- 2 (4½" x 4½" or 6" x 6") squares each fusible web and tear-away fabric stabilizer
- 2 (6" x 6" or 8" x 8") squares each backing and batting
- All-purpose thread to match or contrast with fabrics
- Clear nylon monofilament thread for quilting
- Pattern paper
- Basic sewing tools and supplies

INSTRUCTIONS

1. Prepare frame pieces, fuse to the background fabric and machine-stitch in place referring to the General Instructions.

2. Using the fused square as a pattern, cut one batting and backing piece for each coaster.

3. Place the backing piece right sides together with the stitched framed piece; place batting on top. Stitch all around, leaving an opening on one side for turning.

4. Turn right side out through the opening; press flat. Turn opening edges to the inside and hand-stitch closed.

5. Machine-stitch around the inside edges of the frame design and ⅛" from edge all around to finish. ■

The two top photos show both style B (the first frame cut from the frame fabric) and style C (made using the cut-out center of the frame fabric coasters using the Frame 1 design. The bottom photos are samples of how the Ornate Frames can be used.

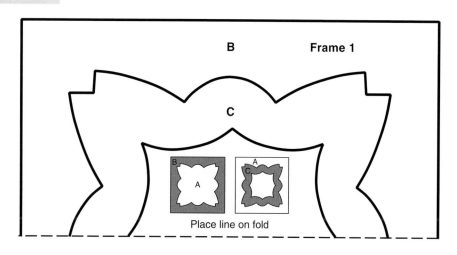

B   Frame 1

C

Place line on fold

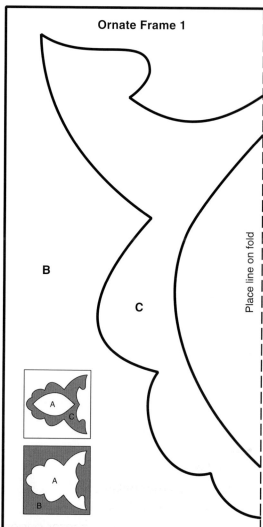

Ornate Frame 1

B

C

Place line on fold

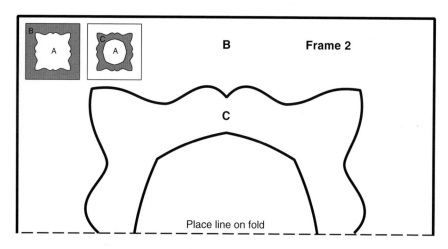

B   Frame 2

C

Place line on fold

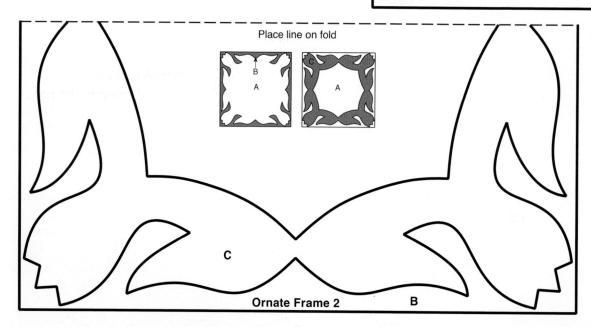

Place line on fold

C

Ornate Frame 2   B

Leisure Time Pursuits

BY PAT HILL

When four blocks are framed and joined, the frames form a pretty design in the center.

PROJECT SPECIFICATIONS
Finished Size: 24" x 24"

MATERIALS
- 2 (12" x 12") A squares each cream solid and cream star print
- 1¼ yards red tonal
- Backing 28" x 28"
- Batting 28" x 28"
- All-purpose thread to match or contrast with fabrics
- Clear nylon monofilament thread for quilting
- Red embroidery floss
- 4 (12½" x 12½") squares freezer paper
- Basic sewing tools and supplies

INSTRUCTIONS
1. Prepare and appliqué the appliqué motifs to two A squares.

2. Transfer and outline-stitch the embroidery designs to the remaining A squares using 2 strands red embroidery floss.

3. Fold each freezer-paper square as shown in Figure 1; transfer the frame design to each folded freezer-paper square. Cut out on traced lines; unfold and iron each shape to the wrong side of the red tonal; cut out, leaving a ³⁄₁₆" seam allowance all around the inside.

Figure 1

4. Turn under the seam allowance onto the freezer paper and iron; remove freezer paper and hand-stitch a frame to each A.

5. Arrange the framed A squares and join to complete the quilt top referring to the project photo; press.

6. Quilt and bind referring to page 6. ■

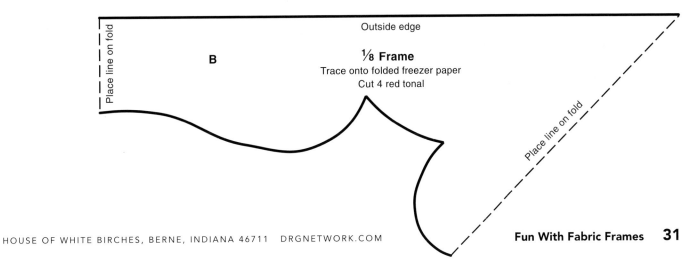

Outside edge

B

⅛ Frame
Trace onto folded freezer paper
Cut 4 red tonal

Place line on fold

Place line on fold

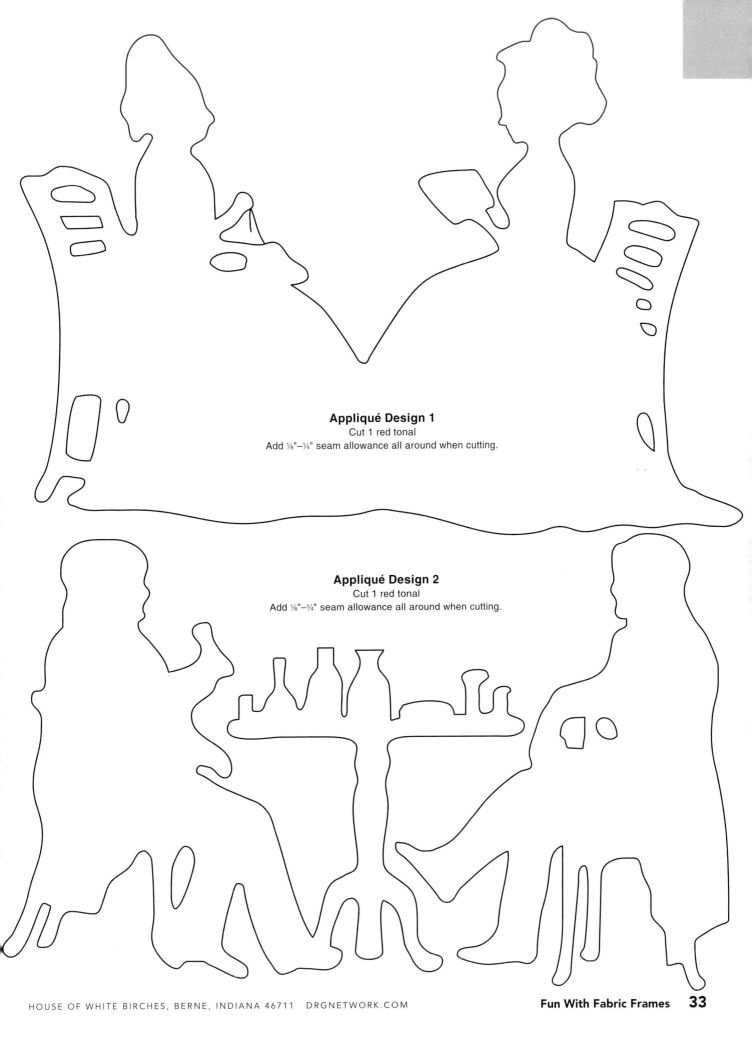

Appliqué Design 1
Cut 1 red tonal
Add ⅛"–¼" seam allowance all around when cutting.

Appliqué Design 2
Cut 1 red tonal
Add ⅛"–¼" seam allowance all around when cutting.

Embroidery Design 1

HOUSE OF WHITE BIRCHES, BERNE, INDIANA 46711   DRGNETWORK.COM

Embroidery Design 2

Halloween Fun

BY JOYCE MORI

This is a super way to make a quick Halloween quilt.

PROJECT NOTES

This wall quilt uses fussy-cut background motifs, which are then surrounded by a frame that serves to highlight the design.

PROJECT SPECIFICATIONS

Finished Size: 19" x 19"

MATERIALS

- 4 (8" x 8") squares each Halloween scenes (A), fusible web and tear-away fabric stabilizer
- 4 (10" x 10") B squares frame fabric
- 4 (2" x 8½") C strips orange print
- 4 (1¼" x 18") D strips orange print
- 1 (2" x 2") E square pumpkin print
- 4 (1¼" x 1¼") F squares pumpkin print
- 88" (1⅛"-wide) black solid binding strip
- Backing 25" x 25"
- Batting 25" x 25"
- All-purpose thread to match or contrast with fabrics
- Clear nylon monofilament thread for quilting
- Pattern paper
- Basic sewing tools and supplies

INSTRUCTIONS

1. Follow the steps in the General Instructions to frame each A square with B using pattern given. **Note:** *The frame pattern is given as one quarter of the square. Trim the blocks to 8½" x 8½".*

2. Sew a C sashing strip between two blocks to make a block row; press seams toward C.

3. Sew the E square between the two remaining C strips; press seams toward C.

4. Join the block rows with the B-C strip to complete the pieced center; press seam toward the B-C strip.

5. Sew an F square to each end of two D strips; press seams toward D. Sew a D strip to opposite sides and D-F strips to the remaining sides of the pieced center to complete the pieced top; press seams toward D and D-F strips.

6. Complete the quilt referring to page 6. ■

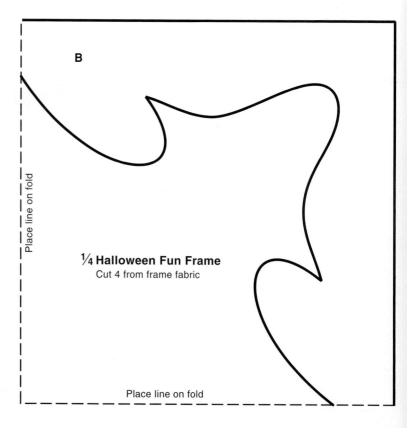

B

¼ **Halloween Fun Frame**
Cut 4 from frame fabric

Place line on fold

Place line on fold

HOUSE OF WHITE BIRCHES, BERNE, INDIANA 46711   DRGNETWORK.COM

Christmas Sleigh

BY JOYCE MORI

Victorian elegance is the theme of this holiday wall quilt.

PROJECT NOTES

Change the theme of this wall quilt using leaves, pumpkins or flowers instead of the sleigh.

PROJECT SPECIFICATIONS

Finished Size: 19" x 13"

MATERIALS

- 21" x 15" A rectangle gold/cream metallic print
- 1 (18" x 12") rectangle each green batik (B), fusible web and tear-away fabric stabilizer
- 1 (17" x 11") rectangle each red tonal and fusible web
- 2 motifs cut from fabric (poinsettia and bow in sample)
- 76" (1⅛"-wide) red tonal binding strip

- 1 each 17" x 11" and 10" x 6" rectangle paper for pattern
- Backing 23" x 17"
- Batting 23" x 17"
- All-purpose thread to match or contrast with fabrics
- Clear nylon monofilament thread for quilting
- Gold embroidery floss
- Pattern paper
- Basic sewing tools and supplies

INSTRUCTIONS

1. Prepare frame pattern as directed on pattern and cut as shown in Figure 1.

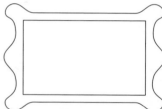

Figure 1

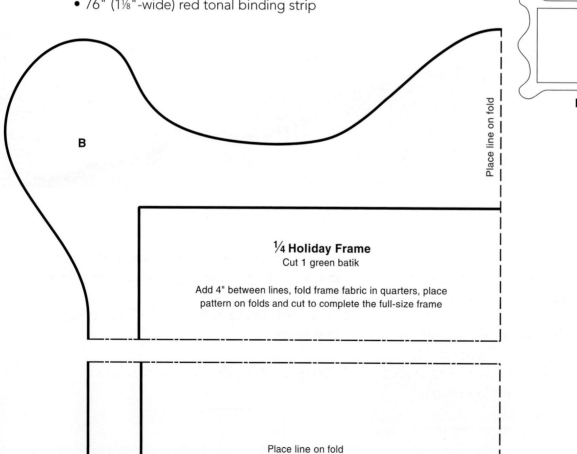

B

Place line on fold

¼ **Holiday Frame**
Cut 1 green batik

Add 4" between lines, fold frame fabric in quarters, place pattern on folds and cut to complete the full-size frame

Place line on fold

2. Refer to the General Instructions to complete the framed background.

3. Center the sleigh shape on the framed background; fuse and appliqué in shape as for frame.

4. Bond fusible web to the wrong side of the chosen fabric motifs; cut out shapes and fuse to the inside of the framed background as desired. Appliqué in place as for sleigh and frame.

Remove fabric stabilizer.

5. Transfer detail lines to sleigh area; stem-stitch along lines using 2 strands gold embroidery floss.

6. Trim background to 19½" x 13½", centering framed area.

7. Complete the quilt referring to page 6. ■

Sleigh
Cut 1 red tonal

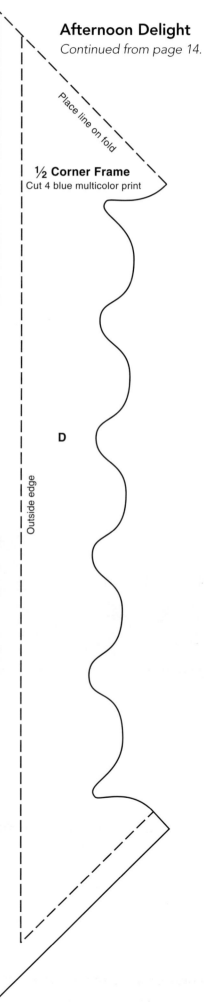

Afternoon Delight
Continued from page 14.

Place line on fold

½ **Corner Frame**
Cut 4 blue multicolor print

Outside edge

D

Christmas Stockings

BY JOYCE MORI

Fussy-cut appliqué motifs from holiday fabrics
are featured in free-form frames in these
holiday stockings.

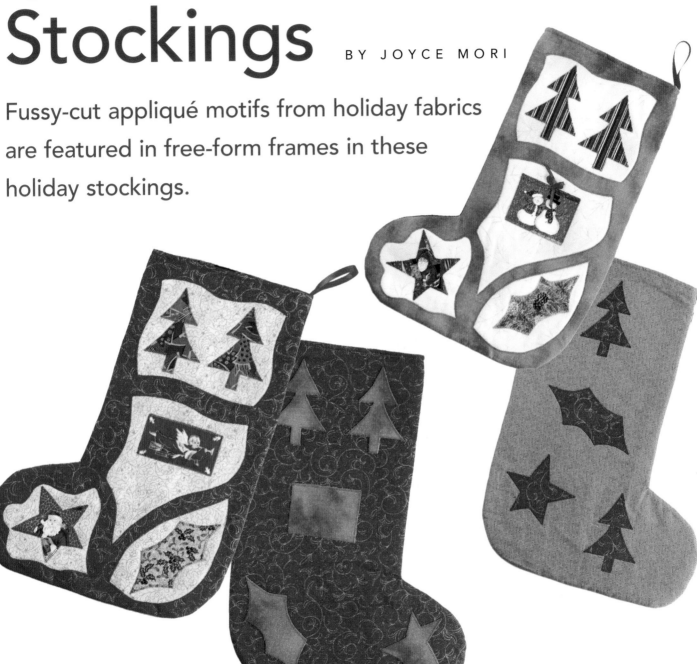

Make a set of Christmas Stockings using two layers of fabric. Cut
openings in the top fabric layer to frame fussy-cut appliqué motifs
such as the trees, stars and leaves shown in the samples. Appliqué
the top layer of fabric in place using the frame method given in the
General Instructions.

A Different View of Monet

BY PAT HILL

A large section of a watercolor print in a Monet style is featured in this quilted art piece. This fabric serves as the background for four large frames with a center frame that is woven in and out of the corner frames. Another frame has been added to border the background fabric creating a quilted art piece.

Recipe Cards

BY JOYCE MORI

Frame a recipe as a gift for the hostess of a party to which you bring a special dish.

PROJECT SPECIFICATIONS

Finished Size: 4" x 4" or 4" x 6"

INSTRUCTIONS

1. Follow the steps in the General Instructions to complete frames for recipe cards using patterns given. ■

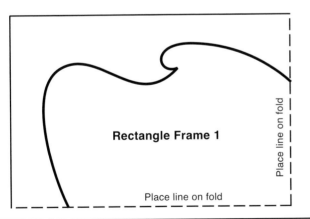

Rectangle Frame 1

Place line on fold

Place line on fold

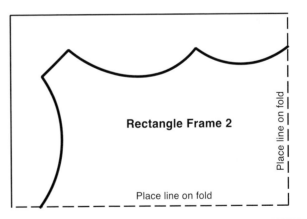

Rectangle Frame 2

Place line on fold

Place line on fold

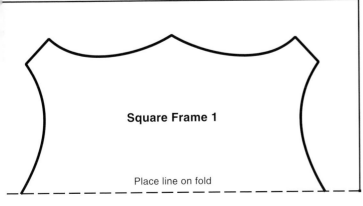

Square Frame 1

Place line on fold

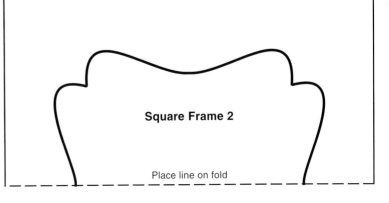

Square Frame 2

Place line on fold

Personalized Totes

BY JOYCE MORI

Make a quick-and-fun personalized tote for yourself and others.

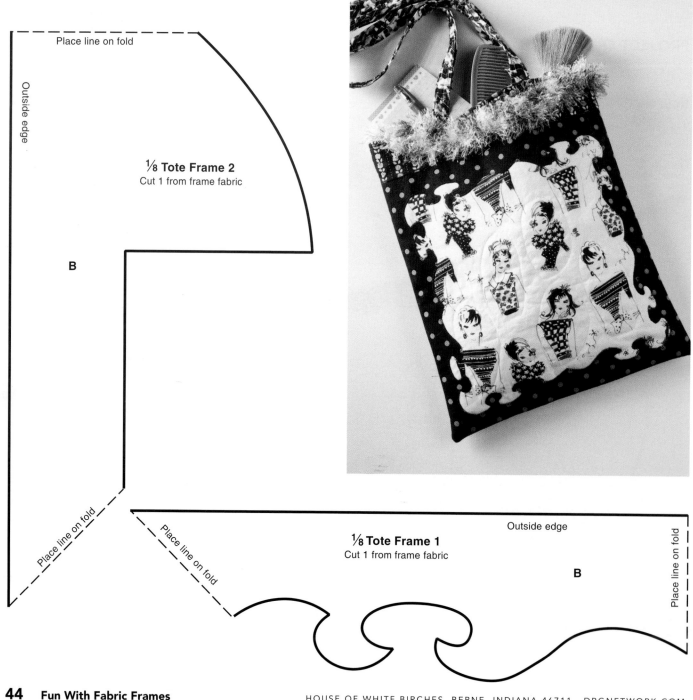

Place line on fold

Outside edge

⅛ **Tote Frame 2**
Cut 1 from frame fabric

B

Place line on fold

Place line on fold

Outside edge

⅛ **Tote Frame 1**
Cut 1 from frame fabric

B

Place line on fold

HOUSE OF WHITE BIRCHES, BERNE, INDIANA 46711   DRGNETWORK.COM

Frame a 12" square of fabric and add a strip to the top and bottom to make the front and back panels for a trendy bag. The bags shown have different fabrics on the fronts and back and include a knit accent around the top edge.

Zigzag Frenzy

BY JOYCE MORI

The edges of the framed fabric show in this zigzag frame design.

PROJECT NOTES

Create a secondary design where the four blocks are joined in this framed piece. Small accent motifs are placed in the corners to emphasize the center design.

PROJECT SPECIFICATIONS

Finished Size: 22" x 22"

MATERIALS

- 4 different 10" x 10" A squares bright prints
- 4 different 8½" x 8½" B squares dark mottleds
- 4 (8½" x 8½") squares each fusible web and tear-away fabric stabilizer
- 2 (5" x 5") C squares each orange and hot pink prints
- 4 (5" x 5") squares each fusible web and tear-away fabric stabilizer
- 2 strips each 1½" x 16½" D and 1½" x 18½" E lime green tonal
- 2 strips each 2½" x 18½" F and 2½" x 22½" G purple tonal
- 100" (1⅛"-wide) purple tonal binding strip
- Backing 26" x 26"
- Batting 26" x 26"
- All-purpose thread to match or contrast with fabrics
- Clear nylon monofilament thread for quilting
- Pattern paper
- Basic sewing tools and supplies

INSTRUCTIONS

1. Prepare and cut frame pattern and corner accent pieces as directed on patterns.

2. Refer to the General Instructions to place and stitch each B frame on an A square referring to Figure 1. Trim the blocks to 8½" x 8½".

Figure 1

3. Join two blocks; press seam in one direction. Repeat and join the rows with seams in opposite directions; press seam in one direction.

4. Referring to Figure 2, sew D to opposite sides and E to the top and bottom; press seams toward strips. Repeat with F and G strips.

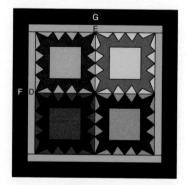

Figure 2

5. Arrange, fuse and stitch a corner accent piece to each corner referring to the General Instructions to complete the top.

6. Complete the quilt referring to page 6. ∎

A narrow stripe fabric was used as the frame fabric for a leaf print. The Native American Pottery Quilt (page 11) shows another way to use a stripe fabric as the frame fabric.

A free-form, wavy-edge circle was cut from the leftover center of the stripe frame. A rectangle was added to the square frame to create a door-knob hanger.

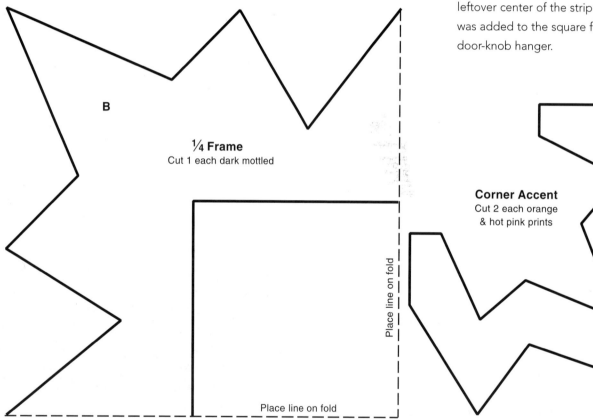

B

¼ Frame
Cut 1 each dark mottled

Place line on fold

Place line on fold

Corner Accent
Cut 2 each orange
& hot pink prints

C

E-mail: Customer_Service@whitebirches.com

HOUSE of WHITE BIRCHES
PUBLISHERS SINCE 1947

Fun With Frames is published by DRG, 306 East Parr Road, Berne, IN 46711, telephone (260) 589-4000. Printed in USA. Copyright © 2007 DRG. All rights reserved. This publication may not be reproduced in part or in whole without written permission from the publisher.

RETAIL STORES: If you would like to carry this pattern book or any other DRG publications, call the Wholesale Department at Annie's Attic to set up a direct account: (903) 636-4303. Also, request a complete listing of publications available from DRG.

Every effort has been made to ensure that the instructions in this pattern book are complete and accurate. We cannot, however, take responsibility for human error, typographical mistakes or variations in individual work.

ISBN: 978-1-59217-203-0
1 2 3 4 5 6 7 8 9

STAFF
Editors: Jeanne Stauffer, Sandra L. Hatch
Managing Editor: Dianne Schmidt
Technical Artist: Connie Rand
Copy Supervisor: Michelle Beck
Copy Editors: Nicki Lehman,
   Mary O'Donnell, Judy Weatherford
Graphic Arts Supervisor: Ronda Bechinski

Graphic Artist: Amy Lin
Art Director: Brad Snow
Assistant Art Director: Nick Pierce
Photography: Tammy Christian, Don Clark,
   Matthew Owen
Photo Stylists: Tammy Steiner,
   Tammy M. Smith